DISCOVER!

CALLING ALL COMMUNITY HEROES!

WHO SAVES PEOPLE IN STORMS?

BY THERESA EMMINIZER

Enslow PUBLISHING

Please visit our website, www.enslow.com.
For a free color catalog of all our high-quality books, call toll free 1-800-398-2504 or fax 1-877-980-4454.

Library of Congress Cataloging-in-Publication Data
Names: Emminizer, Theresa, author.
Title: Who saves people in storms? / Theresa Emminizer.
Description: Buffalo, New York : Enslow Publishing, [2025] | Series: Calling all community heroes! | Includes index. | Audience term: Children
Identifiers: LCCN 2024028851 (print) | LCCN 2024028852 (ebook) | ISBN 9781978542280 (library binding) | ISBN 9781978542273 (paperback) | ISBN 9781978542297 (ebook)
Subjects: LCSH: First responders–Juvenile literature. | Storms–Juvenile literature.
Classification: LCC HV554.3 .E47 2025 (print) | LCC HV554.3 (ebook) | DDC 362.18–dc23/eng/20240731
LC record available at https://lccn.loc.gov/2024028851
LC ebook record available at https://lccn.loc.gov/2024028852

Published in 2025 by
Enslow Publishing
2544 Clinton Street
Buffalo, NY 14224

Designer: Tanya Dellaccio Keeney
Editor: Theresa Emminizer

Photo credits: Cover (background) ASTA DESIGN/Shutterstock.com; cover (speech bubble) mejorana/Shutterstock.com; cover (person) industryviews/Shutterstock.com; cover (storm) Saigh Anees/Shutterstock.com; p. 5 Derek Robbins/Shutterstock.com; p. 7 Frame Stock Footage/Shutterstock.com; p. 9 All Stock Photos/Shutterstock.com; p. 11 Gorodenkoff/Shutterstock.com; p. 13 Peter Rhys Williams/Shutterstock.com; p. 15 VanderWolf Images/Shutterstock.com; pp. 17, 21 michelmond/Shutterstock.com; p. 19 Suzanne Tucker/Shutterstock.com.

Printed in the United States of America

CPSIA compliance information: Batch #CWENS25: For further information contact Enslow Publishing, at 1-800-398-2504.

CONTENTS

BOLDFACE WORDS APPEAR IN WORDS TO KNOW.

WHEN A STORM STRIKES

Snowstorms! Floods! Wild winds! When a storm strikes, or hits, it can be very scary. Luckily, community heroes are here to help. Community heroes are brave people who face many dangers and work hard to keep other people safe.

STORMS CAN BE VERY DANGEROUS, OR UNSAFE.

METEOROLOGISTS

Meteorologists are scientists who study weather. They help predict, or guess based on facts, when a storm is coming and where it will strike. Knowing that a storm is on its way means that people can prepare, or get ready for it.

METEOROLOGISTS USE TECHNOLOGY TO PREDICT STORMS.

SHELTER VOLUNTEERS

When a very strong storm is predicted, sometimes people must evacuate. To evacuate means to move out of an unsafe area. People may go to an **emergency** shelter. It is a safe place for people to stay. Shelter workers are often volunteers. This means they have chosen to help and aren't getting paid for it.

SHELTERS ARE USUALLY TEMPORARY, MEANING THEY'RE ONLY TO BE USED FOR A SHORT TIME.

MEDICAL WORKERS

Medical workers give health care to those in need. Many people can be injured, or harmed, during storms. They may have been caught outside in dangerous weather. Things may fall and hurt people. Medical workers treat people's injuries.

FIRST RESPONDERS ARE THE FIRST PEOPLE WHO SHOW UP TO HELP IN AN EMERGENCY.

FIREFIGHTERS

Firefighters do more than put out fires. They also save people from storms! Firefighters use their lifesaving training and tools to help people in many different **disasters**, such as **hurricanes** and **tornadoes**. Firefighters also help clear away fallen trees and power lines.

THIS FIRE CREW IS RESCUING, OR SAVING, PEOPLE IN A FLOOD.

SEARCH AND RESCUE TEAMS

During storms, families can become separated. People may be lost. Search and rescue (SAR) teams find and aid these people. SAR teams may search in mountains, forests, open water, or under **wreckage** for people who may be trapped or hurt.

SAR TEAMS MAY USE A HELICOPTER DURING A STORM AT SEA.

FEMA

FEMA is the Federal Emergency Management **Agency**. FEMA's job is to help people before, during, and after disasters. FEMA works closely with **local** first responders to organize the emergency response. It also partners with the American Red Cross, a **humanitarian** group.

FEMA WORKERS TRAVEL TO DIFFERENT PLACES, GIVING HELP WHERE IT'S MOST NEEDED.

FRIENDS, NEIGHBORS, AND KIND STRANGERS

Often, the community heroes who save people in storms are simply kind people! Community members who offer shelter, food, water, and care to neighbors do lifesaving work. If there's a power outage during a snowstorm, sheltering in a neighbor's heated house could save someone's life.

DURING A SNOWSTORM, NEIGHBORS WORK TOGETHER TO STAY SAFE.

AFTER THE STORM

Storms wipe out people's homes, leaving them without food, water, or many other things they need to survive, or live. Long after a storm ends, community heroes continue to do their lifesaving work. They feed and shelter people in need and help a community begin again.

THESE SHELTER WORKERS ARE GIVING FOOD AND WATER TO PEOPLE IN HOUSTON, TEXAS.

WORDS TO KNOW

agency: A government department that handles a certain activity.

disaster: An event that causes much suffering or loss.

emergency: An unexpected situation that needs quick action.

humanitarian: Having to do with working for the health and happiness of other people.

hurricane: A powerful storm that forms over water and causes heavy rainfall and high winds.

local: Having to do with a nearby area.

technology: Using science, engineering, and other industries to invent useful tools or to solve problems. Also a machine or method created by technology.

tornado: A violent, destructive whirling wind.

wreckage: The broken pieces left after something has been damaged.

FOR MORE INFORMATION

BOOKS

Bergin, Raymond. *Terrible Storms*. Minneapolis, MN: Bearport Publishing, 2022.

Rossiter, Brienna. *We Need Public Safety Workers*. Lake Elmo, MN: Focus Readers, 2022.

WEBSITES

FEMA
www.fema.gov/pdf/library/pfd.pdf
Read about how you can prepare for a disaster.

Ready
www.ready.gov/evacuation
Know where to go and what to bring in case your family is evacuated during a disaster.

Publisher's note to educators and parents: Our editors have carefully reviewed these websites to ensure that they are suitable for students. Many websites change frequently, however, and we cannot guarantee that a site's future contents will continue to meet our high standards of quality and educational value. Be advised that students should be closely supervised whenever they access the internet.

INDEX